# The Five Marks o

THE M-SERIES are a collection of short, accessible papers and articles from Micah Global, being developed in response to the need for clear, authoritative statements on key themes. They form a foundation of historical and current ideas that contribute to our understanding and practice of integral mission. They aim to promote reflection, dialogue, articulation and action on the major concepts and issues that move us towards transforming mission.

The M-series are an essential resource for practitioners, theologians, students, leaders, and teachers.

# M-Series from im:press

*Titles in print:*

*Integral Mission: Biblical foundations*
by Melba Maggay

*The Five Marks of Mission:*
*Making God's mission ours* by Chris Wright


*In preparation:*

*Towards Transformed Honour* by Arley Loewen

*Paying the Unpaid Debts* by Flip Buys

# The Five Marks of Mission: making God's mission ours

### Chris Wright
International Ministries Director
Langham Partnership

Published by

im:press

An imprint of Micah Global

ISBN: 978-0-9945911-0-4

Typeset in Warnock Pro

Printed and bound by Ingram Spark

# Where should we start?

O NE of the most fertile grounds for disagreement among Christians is our understanding of what is meant by 'mission'. We argue over what it is, who does it the right way, where it should happen, what it includes or excludes, what the immediate or ultimate objectives are, what 'success' looks like, and when we'll achieve it.

Sometimes the cause of so much disagreement is that we tend to have a very human-centred concept of mission. It seems that when we focus primarily on people, whether as the 'target' of mission, or as the agents of mission activity, we end up in the same endless argument over relative needs and priorities. What should holistic mission include? What should a 'missional church' be doing? That kind of discussion does have a proper place, of course, since we should try to think clearly about what we ought to be doing and why. But our proper starting point in defining mission biblically should be first of all the mission of God. What does the Bible tell us about the overarching plan and purpose of God for the whole creation and the human race? For if we have any mission to engage in, it must surely be connected in some way to the mission of the God who created and redeemed us.

# One

# The Mission of God

WHAT then is the great plan and purpose of God? One of the most concise answers to that question is given by Paul. God has 'made known to us the mystery of his will according to his good pleasure, which he purposed in Christ, to be put into effect when the times reach their fulfillment—to bring unity to all things in heaven and on earth under Christ' (Eph. 1:9-10). When Paul speaks of 'God's will', he does not usually mean God's personal guidance for our individual lives, but his 'sovereign' will, God's great cosmic purpose throughout all time and space.

Paul says that God's plan is to bring healing and unity to the whole creation in and through Christ. The mission of God is to redeem the whole of creation, broken by sin and evil, into the new creation, populated by the redeemed from every culture, through the cross and resurrection of Christ. I think that is what Paul meant by 'the whole counsel of God' (Acts 20:27). It is the plan of God from Genesis to Revelation. It includes the whole biblical grand-narrative: Creation – Fall – Redemption – New Creation, centred on and united in Christ.[1]

*The mission of God is to redeem the whole of creation, through the cross and resurrection of Christ.*

Mission, then, is fundamentally the activity of God, driving this whole story forward and bringing it to its glorious conclusion. For this rea-

---

1 This is a conviction that I explore in considerable depth and breadth in *The Mission of God: Unlocking the Bible's Grand Narrative* (InterVarsity Press: 2006).

son, when the Cape Town Commitment of 2010 comes to define the mission to which we are committed, it immediately shifts gear into a summary of the mission of God himself.

> We are committed to world mission, because it is central to our understanding of God, the Bible, the Church, human history and the ultimate future. The whole Bible reveals the mission of God to bring all things in heaven and earth into unity under Christ, reconciling them through the blood of his cross. In fulfilling his mission, God will transform the creation broken by sin and evil into the new creation in which there is no more sin or curse. God will fulfil his promise to Abraham to bless all nations on the earth, through the gospel of Jesus, the Messiah, the seed of Abraham. God will transform the fractured world of nations that are scattered under the judgment of God into the new humanity that will be redeemed by the blood of Christ from every tribe, nation, tongue and language, and will be gathered to worship our God and Saviour. God will destroy the reign of death, corruption and violence when Christ returns to establish his eternal reign of life, justice and peace.Then God, Immanuel, will dwell with us, and the kingdom of the world will become the kingdom of our Lord and of his Christ and he shall reign for ever and ever.[2]

We may well say, 'Hallelujah, Amen!' to that. Praise God for the great mission that he will assuredly accomplish. But this still begs the question: what about us? Who are we, as God's people, and what are we here for? What is our mission? At least the statement above should prepare us to expect a broad answer to that question. For if the Bible shows us that God's great mission is so comprehensive in scope, then the church's mission must also be far-reaching and wide-ranging. Not, of course, in the

---

2 *Cape Town Commitment I.10* https://www.lausanne.org/content/ctc/ctcommitment

sense that we can do all that God does; but in the sense that when God calls us to participate with him in fulfilling God's own great purpose for creation and humanity, he calls us into a very big agenda indeed.

That last sentence also captures the crucial point that *our* mission is to participate with God in *God's* mission. What we do in obedience to the sending and commanding of the Lord Jesus Christ must reflect and embody what God himself is doing, or wills to be done, in God's world. Yes, we are 'sent by God'—that is an essential dimension of biblical mission. But in another sense, mission is 'joining with God', going with him, being called and taken by him, into the places where God is already at work and in the tasks where God is already engaged. God is not an absentee general, issuing orders from heaven, but an active agent, sovereignly working out his purposes in history. With that in mind, let's think about how we might define the mission of the church.

# Two

# The mission of God's people, the church

THERE have been many proposals to define and describe the mission of the church. One that I find helpful was produced by the Anglican Consultative Council in 1984. It was conceived as a mission statement for the worldwide Anglican Communion and was adopted by the Lambeth Conference of bishops in 1988 as the *Five Marks of Mission*. It stated that

'The mission of the church is the mission of Christ

1. To proclaim the good news of the Kingdom

2. To teach, baptise and nurture new believers

3. To respond to human need by loving service

4. To seek to transform unjust structures of society

5. To strive to safeguard the integrity of creation and to sustain the life of the earth.'[3]

---

3 Bonds of Affection-1984 ACC-6 p49, Mission in a Broken World-1990 ACC-8 p101. See: http://www.anglicancommunion.org/ministry/mission/fivemarks.cfm

Since 1984 there has been ongoing debate around the 'five marks', and some modification of the terminology. But the essential thrust of them remains, even under different expressions. For example, the Anglican Board of Mission in Australia recently re-framed them as follows:

Witness to Christ's saving, forgiving, reconciling love for all people

Build welcoming, transforming communities of faith

Stand in solidarity with the poor and needy

Challenge violence, injustice and oppression, and work for peace and reconciliation

Protect, care for and renew life on our planet

http://www.anglicannews.org/news/2013/01/abm-welcomes-change-to-the-marks-of-mission.aspx

These could be summarized in a few words: *evangelism, teaching, compassion, justice, and care of creation*. It is a remarkably comprehensive and holistic list that can be shown to have deep roots in the whole Bible. In fact, all five 'marks' can be considered as ways in which we participate in the mission of God—that is, they are activities where we engage in what God himself does or wills to be done. When we do these things, God is actively participating with us and we with him, for these things are clearly identified in the Bible as passionate concerns of God.

## The Five Marks of Mission

I also believe that all five marks of mission can be linked to the Great Commission, to go and make disciples of all nations (Matt. 28:20) and integrated together around it—*provided* we put at the centre of all of them the opening affirmation of the Great Commission: the Lordship of Christ over all creation.

That last point is essential. All of those five dimensions of mission depend on the Lordship of Christ. So here they are, linked together around the centrality of the gospel truth that Jesus is Lord.

- In evangelism: we proclaim the good news that Jesus Christ is Lord, King and Saviour
- In teaching: we bring people into maturity of faith and discipleship, in submission to Christ as Lord
- In compassion: we follow the example of the Lord Jesus, who 'went about doing good' (Acts 10:38).
- In seeking justice: we remember that the Lord Jesus Christ is the judge of all the earth
- In using and caring for creation: we are handling what belongs to the Lord Jesus Christ by right of creation and redemption.

However, I prefer to keep things simpler and we can do that by grouping four of the five into two pairs, putting evangelism and teaching together, and putting compassion and justice together. That then creates three major missional tasks, or three focal points for our missional engagement: church, society and creation. Our mission, then, includes:

1. _Building the church_ (through evangelism and teaching), bringing people to repentance, faith and obedience as disciples of Jesus Christ.

2. _Serving society_ (through compassion and justice), in response to Jesus sending us 'into the world', to love and serve, to be salt and light, to do good, and to 'seek the welfare' of the people around us (as Jeremiah told the Israelites in Babylon, Jer. 29:7).

3. _Caring for creation_ (through godly use of the resources of creation along with ecological concern and action), fulfilling the very first 'great commission' given to humanity in Genesis 1 and 2.

## Church, Society, Creation

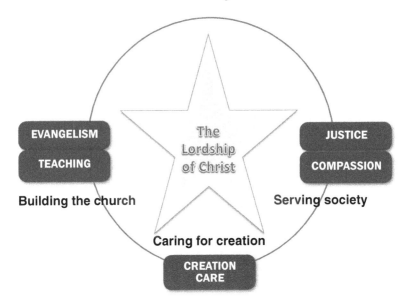

At this point the question may arise, "Doesn't the Great Commission simply tell us to 'go and evangelize the world'?" Well, no actually, it does not just say that. It is not a single command, but several. And it does not start with a command, but with the statement, "All authority in heaven and earth is given to me." Everything flows from that. We build the church because Jesus is Lord of the church. We serve society because Jesus (and not 'Caesar') is Lord of every nation, government and culture, whether acknowledged as such or not. And we care for creation because Jesus is Lord of heaven *and earth*—'the earth is the Lord's and everything in it.' (Ps 24:1) Every dimension of our mission flows from the Lordship of Christ, and from the will and mission of God that the whole world and all creation will come to recognize that fact, and in doing so, will come to know, love, praise and worship our Creator and Redeemer.

This triple scope of mission is fully biblical. The Cape Town Commitment recognizes that all three need to be held together in a truly holistic and integrated understanding of mission.

> Integral mission means discerning, proclaiming, and living out, the biblical truth that the gospel is God's good news, through the cross and resurrection of Jesus Christ, for individual persons, *and* for society, *and* for creation. All three are broken and suffering because of sin; all three are included in the redeeming love and mission of God; all three must be part of the comprehensive mission of God's people.[4]

So let's go around those three main focal points, linking them together within our understanding of integral mission, and seeing how they connect to the Great Commission.

---

4   Cape Town Commitment, I.7a.

# Three

# Building the church: evangelism and teaching

M AKE disciples, baptizing them ... *and* teaching them ..."
This flows immediately and directly from the Lordship of Christ.
For if Jesus of Nazareth is truly Lord and God, then we are summoned
to *become* disciples by submitting to him in repentance and faith, and we
are sent to *make* disciples by bringing others into that same relationship.

## 3.1 Evangelism

Evangelism means 'gospelling' the good news of what God has promised and accomplished through Christ. It means telling the whole story of what God has done, using the whole revealed story of God in Old and New Testaments. It is proclaiming the good news that the God who created the world has acted to save the world from the consequences of human sin and satanic evil; that God has done so through his Son, Jesus of Nazareth, who came in fulfilment of God's promise to Israel and who, as God's appointed Messiah, died for our sins and was raised to life by the power of God; that this same Jesus is now the ascended Lord and that he will return as Judge and King to claim his inheritance with redeemed humanity in the new creation.

Evangelism means that when people respond to this good news of what God has done through Christ, by turning in repentance from whatever false self-constructed and self-serving story they are living in, and putting their faith in Jesus for salvation, we assure them that they have a part in that great biblical story of God's saving purpose for the world, that their sin is forgiven, and they can enjoy a right relationship with God now and eternally. They not only benefit from the saving mission of God, they get to share in it along with us.

And when people make that response, Jesus instructs us to baptize them 'into the name of'—that is, into relationship with —God the Father who loves them, God the Son who died for them, and God the Holy Spirit who dwells within them, bearing his fruit in a life being transformed into the likeness of Christ.

> *Holistic mission integrates everything else that we may do in mission around the gospel*

At this point, it is important to stress that holistic mission does not merely *include* evangelism, but integrates everything else that we may do in mission around the gospel that evangelism declares, since the gospel is the heart and core of God's mission and ours. I have come across two misleading ways of using the phrase 'holistic mission'.

- Sometimes 'holistic mission' is used to mean everything *except* evangelism. It is a kind of 'bag' in which to put all the other ministries: social action, medical mission, poverty relief, community development, environmental action, human rights advocacy, working for peace and reconciliation, etc, etc. It has been used that way even in Lausanne circles, in spite of my protests! But this is wrong and misleading. 'Holistic' means 'the whole thing'. Social action without evangelism is just as non-holistic as is evangelism without social engagement. Holistic mission must include evangelism and not just refer to everything else.

- Sometimes 'holistic mission' is used to mean everything and anything that can be called 'mission' *including* evangelism, but with no integration. Holistic mission becomes like a bag of multi-coloured marbles, in which evangelism is merely one among any number of things that a church might or might not be interested in, or an individual might be gifted in. Mission becomes a smorgasbord of activities, and evangelism is just one option among many. That is also misleading and unbiblical.

Traditionally, many evangelicals have spoken of the primacy of evangelism. They do so because, they argue, evangelism addresses the greatest human need. I do not deny that, but it falls short of the fullness of holistic mission because it does once again frame the issue in human-centred terms. I now prefer to speak of the 'centrality of the gospel', because that phrase reminds us that the gospel is the essential good news of what *God has done* to save the world, and evangelism is the telling of *that* story. We may do a whole lot of things, quite legitimately, in the breadth of many missional callings, but the integrating heart and centre of them all must be the God-centred, God-generated and God-willed reality of the gospel. And we must also insist that 'the gospel' is not merely a personal insurance plan, a ticket to heaven, but is rather the declaration of the whole-Bible story of salvation—the cosmic story of God's redemptive purpose for the whole creation, promised in the Old Testament and accomplished by the death and resurrection of Jesus Christ. It is in evangelism that we tell that story. And it is from that story, and only that story, that all our mission flows.

> 'The gospel' is not merely a ticket to heaven, but is rather the declaration of the whole-Bible story of salvation

So when I speak of the centrality of the gospel and evangelism, I do not mean a centre that makes everything else peripheral—marginal and unimportant, 'out there, far off from the centre'. Rather I mean central in the way that a hub is central to a wheel. A wheel is an integrated functioning object, with a rim or tyre connected to the road. But the full orb of the rim must be connected at every point to the hub through the spokes. In that sense the hub is the integrating centre of all that the wheel is and does. And the hub is connected to the engine, transmitting its power to 'where the rubber hits the road.' There is no point asking 'Which is more important, the hub or the rim?' If you haven't got both integrated together, you haven't got a wheel at all. Both are essential and must function together.

In this analogy for integral or integrated mission, the engine is the dynamic power of the biblical gospel: what God has done in Christ to save the world. The hub is our sharing of that good news. The rim is the embodiment of the gospel in the world in life and work and all our engagement with context and culture (the road). To drive a car, you need integration and connectedness of things that are different from each other in themselves, but cannot really function meaningfully apart from each other—you need the hub of the wheel connected to the engine, and you need the rim of the wheel connected to the road. Otherwise you'll get nowhere! To engage in integral mission you need integration between the historical truth of the gospel, the declaration of that in evangelism, and the embodiment of it in social and contextual engagement with society and creation.

Once again, the Cape Town Commitment seeks to capture this integrated understanding of mission.

> *The integrity of our mission.* The *source* of all our mission is what God has done in Christ for the redemption of the whole world, as revealed in the Bible. Our evangelistic task is to make that good news known to all nations. The *context* of all our mission is the world in which we live, the world of sin, suffering, injustice, and creational disorder, into which God sends us to love and serve for Christ's sake. All our mission must therefore reflect the integration of evangelism and committed engagement in the world, both being ordered and driven by the whole biblical revelation of the gospel of God. [5]

5   The Cape Town Commitment I.10b.

The Lausanne Covenant states it in similar terms:

> Evangelism itself is the proclamation of the historical, biblical Christ as Saviour and Lord, with a view to persuading people to come to him personally and so be reconciled to God ... The results of evangelism include obedience to Christ, incorporation into his Church and responsible service in the world ... We affirm that evangelism and socio-political involvement are both part of our Christian duty. For both are necessary expressions of our doctrines of God and humankind, our love for our neighbour and our obedience to Jesus Christ ... The salvation we proclaim should be transforming us in the totality of our personal and social responsibilities. Faith without works is dead.[6]

Witness also the Micah Declaration of 2001, which set out the nature of integral mission:

> Integral mission is the proclamation and demonstration of the gospel. It is not simply that evangelism and social involvement are to be done alongside each other. Rather, in integral mission our proclamation has social consequences as we call people to love and repentance in all areas of life. And our social involvement has evangelistic consequences as we bear witness to the transforming grace of Jesus Christ. If we ignore the world, we betray the Word of God which sends us out to serve the world. If we ignore the Word of God, we have nothing to bring to the world.[7]

So then,

> Let us keep evangelism at the centre of the fully-integrated scope of all our mission, inasmuch as the gospel itself is the source, content and authority of all biblically-valid mission. All we do should be

6   The Lausanne Covenant, Paragraphs 4 and 5
7   The Micah Declaration on Integral Mission

both an embodiment and a declaration of the love and grace of God and his saving work through Jesus Christ.[8]

## 3.2 Teaching/discipling

"...teaching them to observe all that I have commanded you."

That is, we are to make disciples the way Jesus himself made disciples. It's no good just bringing people to conversion and leaving it at that. The seed needs deep soil and good roots in order to bear fruit. Churches need not only to be planted through evangelism, but also watered through teaching. Both are Great Commission mandates. And both are clearly also God's will for his people. God is at work not only bringing people to faith in Christ, but bringing them to maturity in Christ, through the work of the Holy Spirit within them, with his gifts, power and fruit in their lives. To teach within the church is to join in the process by which God himself brings his people to the fullness of maturity and Christ-likeness. It is another way in which we share in the mission of God.

Teaching is deeply rooted in the Bible. It was an essential part of the way God called, shaped and 'educated' his people Israel in the Old Testament. Professor Andrew Walls has called the Old Testament 'the oldest and longest program of theological education.'[9] For many generations God was teaching his people—through the Torah, Psalms and Wisdom, through priests and prophets—teaching them the truth about God, creation, humanity, sin, redemption, worship, and how to live as a covenant people for the ultimate blessing of the nations.

So it's not surprising that Jesus comes as a teacher. 'Rabbi' they called him. He was so much more, of course, but from the moment he called his disciples to be with him he was teaching, teaching, teaching. Discipleship did not happen overnight.

---

8   The Cape Town Commitment IID.1.e
9   In an unpublished paper delivered at a Mission Leaders' Forum at the Overseas Ministry Studies Centre, New Haven, Connecticut, USA.

When we look at Paul, we notice that teaching was integral to his whole life as a missionary church planter. Often he had to leave a newly-planted church quickly, under threat, but even then he would write to them to encourage and teach. And when he had the opportunity, in Ephesus, he stayed for nearly three years, during which he transformed a group of twelve disciples into a city church with several households and functioning elders. He tells us he had taught them not only all that was helpful for them, but 'the whole counsel of God', i.e. the whole scriptural revelation of God's great plan and purpose (Acts 19-20).

> *Teaching, if we take Jesus seriously, has to be included within our obedience to the Great Commission.*

And when Paul could not personally do the teaching, he ensured that it was done by others who were part of his missionary team, like Timothy and Titus. Or Apollos (from Africa), who was learned in the scriptures, a gifted teacher, who gained further theological education at the home of Priscilla and Aquila (in Asia), and then went to Corinth (in Europe), where he systematically engaged in teaching that included Old Testament hermeneutics, Christology and apologetics (Acts 18:24-28).

Later, when the Christians in Corinth divided into factions boasting loyalty to Paul or Apollos, Paul wouldn't allow it. Yes, Paul was the evangelist church-planter. Yes, Apollos was a theological church-teacher. But they shared a common mission. Paul insists that the evangelist (planter) and the teacher (waterer) have 'one purpose' or a single mission (in Greek, 'they are one'; 1 Cor. 3:5-9).

So teaching within the church in all its forms, including what we would now call theological education, is an intrinsic part of mission. It is not an extra. It is not merely ancillary to 'real mission'. Teaching, if we take Jesus seriously, has to be included within our obedience to the Great

Commission. Once again the Cape Town Commitment hits this particular nail squarely on the head.

> The mission of the Church on earth is to serve the mission of God, and the mission of theological education is to strengthen and accompany the mission of the Church. Theological education serves *first* to train those who lead the Church as pastor-teachers, equipping them to teach the truth of God's Word with faithfulness, relevance and clarity; and *second*, to equip all God's people for the missional task of understanding and relevantly communicating God's truth in every cultural context. Theological education engages in spiritual warfare, as 'we demolish arguments and every pretension that sets itself up against the knowledge of God, and we take captive every thought to make it obedient to Christ.' (2 Corinthians 10:4-5)
>
> Those of us who lead churches and mission agencies need to acknowledge that theological education is intrinsically missional. Those of us who provide theological education need to ensure that it is intentionally missional, since its place within the academy is not an end in itself, but to serve the mission of the Church in the world.[10]

---

10 The Cape Town Commitment II.F.4.

# Serving society: compassion and justice

YOU may ask: Where do compassion and justice figure in the Great Commission? I see it plainly implied in what Jesus says in verse 18: '... teaching them to observe *all that I have commanded you.*' For it is certain that Jesus had plenty of words to say to his disciples about compassion and justice.

But first it is worth hearing the echoes in that phrase itself. It sounds like a very deliberate echo of the way Moses or God addressed the Israelites in the book of Deuteronomy, urging them again and again to 'be careful to observe all that I (or the LORD your God) command you.'[11] And in Deuteronomy it is very clear that what God commanded Israel was to reflect God's own character, by 'walking in his ways'. Read, for example, Deuteronomy 10:12-19. After telling them what God is like and who he most cares for, the text immediately tells the Israelites to do the same —to care for the needy.

> For the Lord your God is God of gods and Lord of lords, the great God, mighty and awesome, who shows no partiality and accepts no bribes. He defends the cause of the fatherless and the widow, and loves the foreigner residing among you, giving them food and clothing. And you are to love those who are foreigners, for you yourselves were foreigners in Egypt (vv. 17-19).

---

11 This would not be surprising, since Jesus meditated deeply on Deuteronomy, quoting from it three times when tempted by Satan in the wilderness.

That is just a single example that could be multiplied many times throughout the Old Testament Scriptures that saturated the mind of Jesus. It is the call to be like God by showing compassion and seeking justice for the poor and needy, for the homeless, the family-less, the land-less—just as God had done for Israel in their need. In the exodus, God had demonstrated the nature and purpose of his mission—compassionate deliverance from oppression. That was the will of God for Israel to experience, and the will of God for Israel to embody in their own social, political and economic life.

So, in the same way and in the same tone of voice, Jesus says to his disciples, 'Your mission is to make disciples and to teach them to obey what I have commanded you, which aligns with all that God has commanded his people from the beginning.'

Even if we only look into Matthew's Gospel, we find this note again and again:

- Matt. 5:6    "Blessed are those who hunger and thirst for justice." The word is often translated 'righteousness', and we have tended to confine that to being right with God. It includes that, of course, but for Jesus and the Old Testament Scriptures, the word meant not only a right relationship with God, but right, just and fair relationships on earth. Blessed are those who hunger and thirst for that, said Jesus.

- Matt. 6:33  "Seek first God's kingdom and his justice/ righteousness."

- Matt. 23:23 "Woe to you, teachers of the law and Pharisees, you hypocrites! You give a tenth of your spices—mint, dill and cumin. But you have neglected the more important matters of the law— justice, mercy and faithfulness. You should have practised the latter, without neglecting the former."

Jesus says that the really heavy stuff (literally 'the weightier matters') of the Torah, are 'justice, mercy and faithfulness'. Again, it is very likely he has in mind the similar triplet found in Micah 6:8, "Do justice, love mercy and walk humbly with your God", or the one in Zechariah 7:9, "Administer true justice; show mercy and compassion to one another."

Out of this shared scriptural background comes Jesus' astonishing word to his disciples, "You are the light of the world" (Matt. 5:14-16). What did he mean by such a sweeping statement? Did he mean that they would be preachers of the truth of the gospel that would bring light to people in the darkness of ignorance and sin? Yes, of course he would have included that in the overall task of the apostolic mission—as Paul explains using the same metaphor in 2 Corinthians 4:4-6. But look again at what Jesus actually stresses when he explains what he means by light: "Let your light shine before others, that they may see *your good deeds* and glorify your Father in heaven." Not 'that they may hear your great testimony', but 'see your good deeds'. They did have a message to preach—of course they did. The good news of the kingdom of God must be shared. But when Jesus talks about 'light' he is speaking of *lives* that are attractive[12] by being filled with goodness, mercy, love, compassion and justice.

> *Jesus says that the really heavy stuff, the weightier matters of the Torah, is 'justice, mercy and faithfulness'*

Once again Jesus is drawing on a strong Old Testament tradition. God had called Israel to be a 'light to the nations', and that included the quality of their lives as a society. Light had a strong ethical and social meaning. Listen to Isaiah, and notice the combination of 'light' and 'righteousness' in the sense explained above. Light shines from people committed to compassion and justice. And, as Isaiah would continue,

---

12 The word translated 'good' is *kalos*, which also means 'beautiful', not just morally upright.

such light, because it reflects the light of God's own presence and glory among his people, will draw the nations—it is missionally attractive (Isa. 60:1-3). It will bring people to glorify the living God. Isn't that what Jesus said?

> Is not this the kind of fasting I have chosen:
>
> to loose the chains of injustice
> >    and untie the cords of the yoke,
>
> to set the oppressed free
> >    and break every yoke?
>
> Is it not to share your food with the hungry
> >    and to provide the poor wanderer with shelter –
>
> when you see the naked, to clothe them,
> >    and not to turn away from your own flesh and blood?
>
> Then *your light* will break forth like the dawn,
> >    and your healing will quickly appear;
> >       then *your righteousness* will go before you ...
>
> if you spend yourselves on behalf of the hungry
> >    and satisfy the needs of the oppressed,
>
> then *your light* will rise in the darkness,
> >    and your night will become like the noonday.
> >                     (Isa. 58:6-8, 10, my italics).

So then, in the Old Testament God commanded Israel to be a people committed to practical, down-to-earth exercise of compassion and justice, in ways that would reflect and embody God's own commitment to those things. And Jesus both endorsed that mandate for his disciples—indeed he radically deepened it—and in the Great Commission commanded them to pass it on to the new disciples they would make ('teaching them to obey all that I have commanded you'). Both in their life as a community of disciples, and in their mission of making disciples, they must reflect the character of the God who cares for the poor and needy, who defends the cause of the widow and orphan.

And they did.

We know, of course, about the exciting story of the mission of the early church, spreading in all directions through evangelism and church-planting. But we should not overlook how the apostles and those first little communities of believers showed a strong commitment to this other dimension of the Great Commission—obeying what Jesus himself had taught about social and economic compassion and justice.

> *The earliest community of Jesus-followers in Jerusalem sought to give their spiritual unity a practical application in economic mutuality*

Luke tells us twice that the earliest community of Jesus-followers in Jerusalem sought to give their spiritual unity a practical application in economic mutuality (Acts 2:44-45; 4:32-38). They did not believe there should be any poor persons among them while they had the ability to do something about it. Whether consciously or not, they were fulfilling another word of God in Deuteronomy (Acts 4:34 is almost word for word the same as the Greek translation of Deut. 15:4).

Paul's first missionary journey with Barnabas was actually not when they were sent by the church in Antioch to preach the gospel in Asia Minor (Acts 13), but when they had been sent earlier by that same church to bring famine relief to needy believers in Jerusalem (Acts 11:27-30). That memory must have been part of the reason for Paul's sustained effort to raise funds among the gentile churches in Greece for the support of the poor in Judea. Clearly Paul had taught those new disciples that responsibility, such that they even pleaded for the privilege of sharing in it (2 Cor. 8-9). In fact, at a most significant moment in Paul's missionary career, when he was granted acceptance ('the right hand of fellowship') among the Jerusalem apostles for the gospel message he was preaching, he adds this revealing comment, showing that Paul included care for the poor as an integral part of his missionary work: "All they asked was that we should continue to remember the poor, the very thing I had been eager to do all along" (Gal. 2:10).

Other passages give the same emphasis on practical economic and social compassion, leaving us in no doubt about the importance of this kind of obedience: 1 Timothy 6:17-19; James 2:14-17; 1 John 3:17-18. Jesus and the apostles would all have agreed with the simple affirmation of Proverbs 29:7, "The righteous person cares about justice for the poor, but the wicked have no such concern."

Once again, the Cape Town Commitment provides a rich biblical foundation for this dimension of mission, stating clearly that such actions are nothing less than a sharing in the mission of God, for God wills these things to be done and mandates them as part of the mission of God's people.

> *We love the world's poor and suffering.* The Bible tells us that the Lord is loving toward all he has made, upholds the cause of the oppressed, loves the foreigner, feeds the hungry, sustains the fatherless and widow.[13] The Bible also shows that God wills to do these things through human beings committed to such action. God holds responsible especially those who are appointed to political or judicial leadership in society,[14] but all God's people are commanded—by the law and prophets, Psalms and Wisdom, Jesus and Paul, James and John—to reflect the love and justice of God in practical love and justice for the needy.[15]
> *Such love for the poor* demands that we not only love mercy and deeds

---

13  Psalms 145:9, 13, 17; 147:7-9; Deuteronomy 10:17-18
14  Genesis 18:19; Exodus 23:6-9; Deuteronomy 16:18-20; Job 29:7-17; Psalms 72:4, 12-14; 82; Proverbs 31:4-9; Jeremiah 22:1-3; Daniel 4:27
15  Exodus 22:21-27; Leviticus 19:33-34; Deuteronomy 10:18-19; 15:7-11; Isaiah 1:16-17; 58:6-9; Amos 5:11-15, 21-24; Psalm 112; Job 31:13-23; Proverbs 14:31; 19:17; 29:7; Matthew 25:31-46; Luke 14:12-14; Galatians 2:10; 2 Corinthians 8-9; Romans 15:25-27; 1 Timothy 6:17-19; James 1:27; 2:14-17; 1 John 3:16-18

of compassion, but also that we do justice through exposing and opposing all that oppresses and exploits the poor.[16] 'We must not be afraid to denounce evil and injustice wherever they exist.'[17]

Integral mission is, I think, nothing more than putting flesh on the phrase which Paul uses to summarize his whole missional effort among all nations, at the beginning and end of Romans: 'the obedience of faith'. We are called to the integration of faith and works, of word and deed, of the proclamation and demonstration of the gospel.

16 *The Cape Town Commitment* I.7.c
17 *Lausanne Covenant*, 5.

# Five

# Caring for creation

W E could in fact have started here with creation, since it's where Jesus starts in the Great Commission. As I said earlier, the Great Commission does not begin with a command but with an affirmation, "All authority in heaven and earth is given to me." That combination 'heaven and earth' is the typical scriptural way of referring to the whole of creation. It's not only where Jesus starts, it's also where the Bible starts (Genesis 1:1), and where the Bible ends, with a new heaven and new earth - the new creation (Revelation 21-22). The whole mission of God in the Bible story runs from creation to new creation, and Jesus stands at the centre of it, claiming to be Lord over it all. Jesus is not just 'up in heaven'. Jesus is Lord of heaven *and earth*.

Deuteronomy again provides the backdrop to the amazing claim that Jesus makes in Matthew 28:18. Listen to Moses talking to the Israelites about their God: "Acknowledge and take to heart this day that the Lord is God in heaven above and on the earth below. There is no other" (Deut. 4:39).

YHWH, the LORD God of Israel, is God of heaven and earth: the whole creation. This is a truth about God that the Old Testament repeats all over the place, especially in the Psalms. Jesus, standing on the Mount of Ascension, calmly takes that truth about the God whom all his followers knew and worshipped, and claims it for himself. Not surprisingly Matthew records that when they met Jesus there, 'they worshipped him'— though he also points out with frank honesty that some doubted. They now knew that as they met with the crucified and risen Christ they were in the presence of the living God, creator of heaven and earth.

Whatever our mission may include as we obey the Great Commission in multiple ways, it presupposes that Jesus is Lord of creation, that the earth belongs to him. He is the landlord and we are his tenants. The earth is his property and we are stewards of it, accountable to him for what we do on and with it.

Paul, in his usual way, expands this cosmic, creational truth about Christ in one of the most amazing passages he ever wrote. Read Colossians 1:15-20 in full. Here is just an extract. Notice how many times Paul refers to 'heaven and earth', or to 'all things' —which was another Jewish way of referring to the whole created universe.

> The Son is the image of the invisible God, the firstborn over all creation. For in him all things were created: things in heaven and on earth ... all things have been created through him and for him. He is before all things, and in him all things hold together ... God was pleased to have all his fullness dwell in him, and through him to reconcile to himself all things, whether things on earth or things in heaven, by making peace through his blood, shed on the cross.

The whole universe, including our planet Earth, was created by and for Christ, is sustained in existence by Christ, belongs to Christ as his inheritance, and has been redeemed by Christ through the cross. The same cosmic truth is stated in different ways in John 1 and Hebrews 1. The mission of God, accomplished through Christ, is creational, cosmic, and universal in its scope. God willed, in Genesis 1 and 2, that we should rule, use, keep and care for the earth. And God wills, throughout the Bible right up to Revelation 21-22, that the earth itself will be redeemed, for God's glory and ours, rightly and legitimately combined in the new creation (note the combination in Rev. 21:23-26).

So if the earth we live on is the property of Jesus, belonging to him by right of creation and redemption, we cannot separate our personal submission to Jesus as Lord from the way we think about, and act upon, the earth. Godly use and careful stewardship of the resources of the earth, along with specific ecological advocacy and action, are legitimate dimensions of Christian mission. Christian mission cannot exclude our primal human mission, which was to exercise godly rule over creation by serving and keeping it (Gen. 1:26-28, combined with Gen. 2:15).

> The earth is created, sustained and redeemed by Christ (Colossians 1:15-20; Hebrews 1:2-3) We cannot claim to love God while abusing what belongs to Christ by right of creation, redemption and inheritance. We [as Christians] care for the earth and responsibly use its abundant resources, not according to the rationale of the secular world, but for the Lord's sake. If Jesus is Lord of all the earth, we cannot separate our relationship to Christ from how we act in relation to the earth. For to proclaim the gospel that says 'Jesus is Lord' is to proclaim the gospel that includes the earth, since Christ's Lordship is over all creation. Creation care is a thus a gospel issue within the Lordship of Christ.
>
> *Such love for God's creation* demands that we repent of our part in the destruction, waste and pollution of the earth's resources and our collusion in the toxic idolatry of consumerism. Instead, we commit ourselves to urgent and prophetic ecological responsibility. We support Christians whose particular missional calling is to environmental advocacy and action, as well as those committed to godly fulfilment of the mandate to provide for human welfare and needs by exercising responsible dominion and stewardship.[18]

It is baffling to me that there are so many Christians, including sadly (and especially) those who claim to be evangelicals, for whom this

---

18 The Cape Town Commitment I.7.a.

matter of creation-care, or ecological concern and action, is weak and neglected at best, and even rejected with hostile prejudice at worst. It seems to me that the reason for this is a very defective theology of creation among contemporary evangelicals. To put it bluntly, some people seem to possess damaged Bibles, in which the first two and last two pages have got mysteriously torn off. They start at Genesis 3, because they know all about sin; and they end at Revelation 20, because they know all about the day of judgment. They have their personal solution to the sin problem and their personal security for the day of judgment, provided of course by the death and resurrection of Jesus. Praise God, I believe that too. But the Bible has a much bigger story, the story of the whole creation, within which my personal salvation fits. And the Lordship of Christ spans the whole story. So I need to see him as Lord of my physical environment as well as my spiritual salvation, and behave as his disciple in relation to both.

> *Some people seem to possess damaged Bibles, in which the first two and last two pages have got torn off*

There is no space here to explore the full biblical teaching on creation that makes it entirely legitimate to include creation care within the spectrum of Christian mission. Elsewhere I have provided such a survey of the goodness, the glory and the goal of creation.[19]

---

19  See *The Mission of God*, ch. 12; *Old Testament Ethics for the People of God* (IVP: 2004), ch. 4; and *The Mission of God's People* (Zondervan: 2010), ch. 3.

# So what?

S O WHAT are the implications we might take from this survey of five marks of mission, or three focal points of mission, in relation to the Great Commission? Three points seem to follow.

## 1. God's whole mission is for God's whole church (but everybody can't do everything)

Mission is not a specialist activity for a few professionals (missionaries or mission partners). The church as a whole exists for the sake of God's mission. As has been said, it is not so much the case that God has a mission for the church (to be carried out by a few church-paid professionals), as that God has the church for his mission. The whole church is, in that sense, missional.[20] Everything the church is and does should be connected in some way to our very reason for existence as the people of God in the first place, which is to serve the mission of God for the ultimate glory of God. That is why I dislike the much-abused saying, 'If everything is mission, nothing is mission'. Usually that arises from a fear that if everything a church does is *described* as 'mission', then there will be no special category left for evangelism and sending out missionaries. I hope it is clear from what I said above about the centrality of the gospel and the evangelism that proclaims it, that I am utterly

---

20 A Danish friend of mine, Birger Nygaard, once commented that he found the expression 'missional church' redundant. It sounds, he said, like 'female woman'. If it isn't female, it isn't a woman. Likewise, if it isn't missional, it isn't church. It may be a bunch of people doing religious things together, but if they aren't committed to God's mission in the world, they have (quite literally) lost the plot.

committed to the importance of both those things. But they simply are not the whole of what I believe the Bible includes in the mission of the church, in the sense of all that God has called the church into existence for. It would be more accurate, biblically, to simply say, 'if everything is mission, everything is mission.' The whole church is called to participate in the whole mission of God.

> The church is missional by definition, so all Christians are missional by calling

However, don't be overwhelmed! It is not a case of everybody doing everything, but everybody being intentional about *some*thing, according to the gifting and leading of God. Sometimes people say, after a sermon or lecture about holistic mission, 'You talk about all these different kinds of mission, but there's only one of me. I can't do all that!' To which my reply is, 'I expect God thought of that too, which is why he created the church.' It takes the whole church to engage in God's whole mission.

## 2. The whole church's mission includes every church member (but we have different callings and sendings)

If the whole church exists for God's mission, then so do all its members. The church is missional by definition, so all Christians are missional by calling. We need to radically challenge the mistaken paradigm that only *some* members are 'mission partners'. What does that make the rest of us? Non-mission partners? Sleeping partners? Now of course, usually by 'mission partners' we mean those who are supported and sent by the church and have gone overseas or into some other kind of cross-cultural mission. Then let's call them that: 'cross-cultural mission partners', or 'international mission partners', and not give the impression that mission is not for the rest of us. As Hugh Palmer, Rector of All Souls, Langham Place, said one Sunday: "This church sends out 1,500 mission partners every week—and a few of them are serving abroad." He was implying, of course, that the majority of the congregation every week were entering the 'mission field' of the world immediately outside the church doors, living and working there in their everyday work and callings. The mission field is wherever faith meets unbelief, wherever the kingdom of God in a believer's life encounters the kingdom of this world. That is the front-line of mission. And that could be next door as much as in the next continent.

We need to distinguish between the general missional calling that all of us share, and the specific giftings and callings that God will lay on different ones according to his sovereign grace. All of us are to be ready to bear witness to our faith, but some are specifically gifted as evangelists. All of us are to 'let the word of Christ dwell in you richly as you teach and admonish one another', but some are specifically gifted as teachers. All of us are to be ready to do acts of kindness and speak up for what is just and

> *We have to break the ingrained habit of thinking in two spheres — the secular and the sacred*

right, but some are specifically called to work in political and judicial advocacy, or in tackling global poverty, hunger and disease. All of us should live responsibly in our use and care of creation, but some are called and equipped to pursue environmental biology and do ecologically appropriate scientific research and advocacy.

## 3. Every member's mission includes the whole of life (there is no secular-sacred divide)

If the previous point calls for a change in our paradigm of the church's conception of mission, then this point calls for a change in our personal perspective on life. We have to break the ingrained habit of thinking in two spheres—the secular and the sacred. It has become such a dominating paradigm that we are scarcely conscious of it. It just seems the way things are. There is a 'religious' part of life that God is interested in—church, Christian activities, worship and prayer, evangelism, etc. And there is the rest of life, where most of us spend most of our time—work, family, leisure. And we assume that the whole point of the second sphere is only to give us a bit of money and spare time to do whatever we can to 'support' the first sphere (where the really keen Christians live, as people in church-paid 'full-time ministry').

This is a toxic and demoralizing divide. People are left thinking that what they spend most of their time doing (working in the 'secular' world) has no value to God or for eternity, while they can only give spare time and some money to the one thing that they suppose God really cares about.

But the Great Commission begins by telling us that Jesus is Lord of all of life within his whole creation. Jesus is Lord of the workplace and the family, Lord of the streets and the skies, Lord of schools and slums, Lord of hospitals and housing, Lord of governments, business, academia, sport and culture, Lord of all time and space.

So the discipleship and mission that Jesus calls us into is for the whole of life. If Jesus is Lord of heaven and earth then there is no place, no job, no vocation, no day or night, no part of life at all, that is exempt from the rest of what he says in the Great Commission and all that it refers back to in the rest of the Gospel.

Mission is not an agenda, to be tackled by people assigned to 'do it for the rest of us'. Mission is the mode of existence for the whole life of every member of the whole church.

 micah

MICAH is a global network and movement of Christian organizations and individuals, committed to integral mission as expressed through their response in ministries including relief, rehabilitation, development, creation care, justice, and peacemaking.

Established in 2001, Micah now has over 720 members in 91 countries.

Our vision inspires us towards the realization of communities living life in all its fullness, free from extreme poverty, injustice or conflict. Grounded in the Gospel, and becoming agents of change in our communities, we work to do this in three ways:

- being a catalyst for transforming mission through the promotion of integral mission

- working as a movement towards a united response to advocating for poverty reduction, justice, equality, reconciliation, safety and well-being for all

- having fellowship as a network, providing a platform for shared learning, corporate reflection and action, and facilitation of an information provision hub

Our motivating call to action is captured in Micah 6:8:

**What does the Lord require of you? To act justly, and to love mercy, and to walk humbly with your God.**

Find us at http://www.micahglobal.org

Lightning Source UK Ltd.
Milton Keynes UK
UKHW020616070619

343999UK00007B/1014/P